Celebrate
Sikh Festivals

Series editor: Jan Thompson

John Coutts

First published in Great Britain by
Heinemann Publishers (Oxford) Ltd
Halley Court, Jordan Hill, Oxford OX2 8EJ

MADRID ATHENS PARIS FLORENCE PRAGUE
WARSAW PORTSMOUTH NH CHICAGO
SAO PAULO SINGAPORE TOKYO MELBOURNE
AUCKLAND IBADAN GABORONE
JOHANNESBURG

Designed by Sue Clarke
Colour reproduction by Track QSP

Printed and bound in Hong Kong

99 98 97 96 95
10 9 8 7 6 5 4 3 2 1

ISBN 0 431 06952 2

British Library Cataloguing in Publication Data
Coutts, John
  Sikh Festivals. – (Celebrate Series)
  I. Title II. Series
  294.636

Acknowledgements
The Publishers would like to thank the following for
permission to reproduce photographs.

Mike Goldwater/Network: p.4; Christine Osborne Pictures:
p.5; Ann & Bury Peerless: p.6; Keith Wyncoll: p.7;
Format Photographers: p.7; Ann & Bury Peerless: p.8;
Twin Studio/Amrit & Rabindra Singh: p.11; Ann & Bury
Peerless: p.12; Twin Studio/Amrit & Rabindra Singh: p.13;
Christine Osborne Pictures: p.14; Judy Harrison/Format
Photographers: p.15; Denis Doran/Network Photographers:
p.16; Andes Press Agency: p.17; John Coutts: p.18;
Ann & Bury Peerless: p.19; John Coutts: p.20; Andes Press
Agency: p.22; Sally & Richard Greenhill: p.23; Derek Brown:
p.25; Twin Studio/Amrit & Rabindra Singh: p.26;
Judy Harrison/Format Photographers: p.27; The Hutchison
Library: p.30; Judy Harrison/Format Photographers: p.31;
Christine Osborne Pictures: p.32; Judy Harrison/Format
Photographers: p.33; Keith Wyncoll: p.34; Keith Wyncoll:
p.35; Format Photographers: p.36; Twin Studio/Amrit &
Rabindra Singh: p.37; Ann & Bury Peerless: p.38;
Twin Studio/Amrit & Rabindra Singh: p.39; Twin Studio/Amrit
& Rabindra Singh: p.40; Twin Studio/Amrit & Rabindra Singh:
p.41; Keith Wyncoll: p.42; The Hutchison Library: p.43

Greetings cards on p.21 reproduced courtesy of The Sikh
Missionary Society U.K. (Regd) Southall

Cover photograph Format Photographers/Judy Harrison

Our thanks to Denise Cush of Bath College of Higher
Education for her comments in the preparation of this
book.

The author would like to thank the following for help in the
preparation of this book:
Guru Nanak Sports Club, Gravesend; Hardish Singh;
Jugnu Bhangra Dance Group; Joginder Singh Toor;
Keith Wyncoll; Nasib Cheema; Shaminder Singh Bedi;
Surinder Dhinsa; Virdee Stores, Gravesend.

J200

Contents

The Sikh religion

This unit tells you who Sikhs are and what they believe.

A *Sikh boy in England.*

Amardip is a Sikh. He lives in England. The first thing people notice is that he keeps his hair tied up on top of his head. This is to keep it clean and tidy. Sikhs are not supposed to cut their hair. They let it grow long as a sign that they want to serve God and obey his teaching. The work 'Sikh' means 'disciple' – someone who obeys God.

Surinder is a Sikh, too. She lives in India, where the Sikh religion began about 500 years ago. It was founded by a good and holy man called Guru Nanak. '**Guru**' means 'teacher'. Sikhs recognize ten special teachers: the 'Ten Gurus', who have taught them about God and how to live.

*A Sikh
girl in India.*

Where do Sikhs live?

Most Sikhs live in a part of India called the Punjab. 'Punjab' means 'Five Rivers'. Amardip's parents came to England from the Punjab and the family talk Punjabi at home. One day he hopes to visit India and see his family and friends. He would like to see some of the famous places of Sikhism, such as the Golden Temple in **Amritsar**.

Nowadays many Sikhs have gone to live in other countries, such as Great Britain, Canada and the United States. Surinder is always pleased to get an air letter from her cousins in faraway countries. She would like to go to America and visit them.

What do Sikhs believe?

Sikhs believe in One True God. A Sikh must not worship anything or anyone else. God is very great, mysterious and wonderful – hard to know and understand. But Sikhs believe that they can find out about God from the teaching of the Ten Gurus.

Sikhs also believe that people should be friends, work hard and help each other. Since everybody is special and wonderful, nobody should think they are better than anybody else!

The Ten Gurus used to make up beautiful songs in praise of God. These songs – and others, too – were included in the holy book of the Sikhs: the **Guru Granth Sahib**.

Amardip and Surinder enjoy the special religious festivals when Sikhs sing together, pray together and feast together. This book will tell you about them.

A Sikh prayer

*'Wonderful to me are Your ways
In all creation shines Your light –
   You who are light!
In all creation shines Your
   brightness – You who are light!'*

(From the hymn Sohila – Nit-Nem page 127, simplified.)

Festivals – fun and faith!

This unit describes the main festivals celebrated by Sikhs.

A religious festival is like a party, and it also gives people the chance to pray. It teaches them what to believe and why. Festivals unite old and young people. They bring people together from all parts of the world.

The festivals of Sikhism began in India. They celebrate the work of the **Gurus**, whose words are recorded in the holy book, the **Guru Granth Sahib**. The main points of a festival are the same, whether you live in the town or the country, in India or overseas.

Guru Gobind Singh.

Guru Nanak's birthday

Guru Nanak's birthday is celebrated in November. He was born in 1469 in the village of **Talwandi**, which is now in Pakistan. He was the first Sikh Guru; he taught people to serve the One True God and help others.

Guru Gobind Singh's birthday

Guru Gobind **Singh**'s birthday is celebrated in December. He was the Tenth Guru, born in 1666. He set up the **Khalsa**, the world-wide community of the Sikhs.

Baisakhi

Baisakhi is celebrated in April. For Sikhs it is the most important festival. It is the Indian New Year. In the Punjab, where Sikhism began, it is the Harvest Festival. It is the day when Guru Gobind Singh set up the Khalsa, the Sikh community.

Guru Arjan compiled the Scriptures. Sikhs present a public reading of the whole of their holy book when they celebrate festivals.

Hola Mohalla

Hola Mohalla is celebrated in February or March. It reminds everyone that Guru Gobind Singh taught the Sikhs to keep fit, to behave well and to be ready for battle.

Guru Arjan

The martyrdom of Guru Arjan is remembered in October or November. He was the Fifth Guru, and he compiled the holy book of the Sikhs. He was cruelly killed because he would not deny his faith.

Divali

Divali, the Festival of Light, is observed in October or November. Houses are lit up with oil lamps, candles and coloured lights. There are fireworks and family feasts. Sikhs often tell how the Sixth Guru, Har Gobind, won freedom on this day (see pages 40–1).

Divali, the Festival of Light.

Guru Nanak's birthday (1)

This unit tells you about Guru Nanak's early life.

> **Here is a story which my teacher, Mrs Cheema, told me on Guru Nanak's birthday.**
> – *Joginder*

On 15 April in the year 1469 a very special child was born in the village of **Talwandi**. Baby Nanak never cried – not even when he was born or when he was hungry. There was a smile on his face and his eyes sparkled with joy. Everyone who saw him loved him. In India people often study the stars to discover what the future of a new baby will be. But when the local **astrologer** came, he bowed down and touched the new baby's feet. Young Nanak, he said, would be a special king, loved and respected by all. This came true, because Nanak taught people the truth about God, so they called him '**Guru**' or 'teacher'.

Guru Nanak.

Nanak the student

When Guru Nanak went to school, it only took him a few days to become good at reading and writing. In those days children wrote with chalk on wooden boards. Nanak's teacher asked him to copy out the alphabet, but the boy did more: he took each letter in turn and used it to begin a line of a poem in praise of God. This is called an 'acrostic'.

Nanak also learned **Sanskrit**, the ancient language of India. This meant that he could read the holy books of the **Hindu** faith. He also studied Persian, which was spoken by kings and important people in those days. It is said that he made an acrostic poem in Persian, too. It began something like this –

Letter Alif (A) *Always remember God.*

Letter Be (B) *Be humble before everyone: call nobody bad.*

Letter Te (T) *True sorrow for doing wrong will save you from grief.*

– and so on until he had finished the whole alphabet.

Guru Nanak knew this prayer in Sanskrit.

ॐ

भूर्भुवस्सुवः
तत् सवितुर्वरेण्यं
भर्गो देवस्य धीमहि
धियो योनः प्रचोदयात्

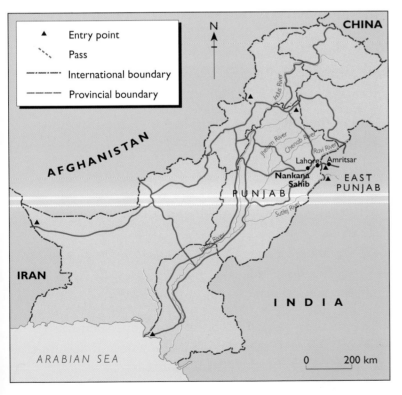

Nanak spent so much time praying and thinking about God that his father became very worried. He sent his son out to the fields to look after cattle. But Nanak fell asleep, and the cattle ate grass from a neighbour's land. The owners complained, but young Nanak said: 'Don't be angry; God will bless your field'. Sure enough, when they came to look at it again, the field was green and flourishing.

Guru Nanak said:

> 'As fragrance dwells in a flower
> And reflection in a mirror,
> So does God dwell in every soul:
> Seek him, therefore, in yourself!'

A map showing the location of Talwandi, now called Nankana Sahib.

Guru Nanak's birthday (2)

This unit tells you about Nanak's vision of God.

When Nanak grew up, he got work as a storekeeper to the Governor. It looked as if he could become a high official in the government. He was provided with food as part of his salary, but he would give most of it away. Part of his job was to weigh out provisions. Sometimes he would get to the number 13 – 'tera' in his language. 'Tera' also means 'yours', and Nanak would say it over and over again: 'Yours … yours … yours … ' meaning 'I am yours, O God!'.

" **Here is another story that teacher told us. "**
– *Parvinder*

Nanak's vision

Every morning, while it was still dark, Nanak would go to bathe in the River **Bein**. Once he did not come back for three days, and most people thought that he had drowned. But Nanak reported that he had been in the forest, where he had enjoyed a vision of God. He said he had been taken into the presence of God himself. There he had been given a cup of nectar (sweet water) and God had said to Nanak: 'I am with you. I have made you happy. Go and repeat my name and make others do the same.'

Nanak then sang this song, accompanied by music from heaven:

> *If I were to become a bird and fly to a hundred heavens,*
> *If I were to vanish from human beings and never eat or drink,*
> *If my ink were never to run out, and I could move my pen like the wind,*
> *I should not be able to express your worth.*

A voice then said: 'O Nanak, you have seen my power'. After this Nanak said the words that sum up the Sikh religion: the **Mool Mantar**.

Guru Nanak bathing in the River Bein, and being taken into the presence of God.

Mool Mantar

IK ONKAAR

SAT NAAM

KARTA PURKH

NIR BHAU

NIR VAIR

AKAL MOORAT

AJOONI

SAIBHANG

GUR PARSHAAD

There is one God

Whose name is truth

Who creates

Who is without fear

Who is without hate

Who does not die

Who is not born

Who is the light

Who is known by the kindness of the true Guru

Nanak gave up his well paid job and became a wandering preacher. Some said he was mad, but others recognized him as a prophet.

Guru Nanak's birthday (3)

This unit tells you how Guru Nanak brought God's message to the people.

Nanak's helpers

When **Guru** Nanak was born, there were two main religions in India. Most people were Hindus, but there were also many Muslims. Unfortunately, they did not always agree. Guru Nanak wanted to find and teach the truth about God. He chose two helpers, a **Hindu** called Bala and a **Muslim** musician called Mardana. He wanted to show that people who followed different religions could be friends. Mardana composed many of the tunes for Guru Nanak's songs. Some of these will certainly be sung in the **gurdwara** (Sikh temple) on Nanak's birthday.

Nanak's travels

Guru Nanak travelled far and wide, telling people his message about God. He made four great journeys, visiting India, Sri-Lanka, Iran and Arabia. Some of the people seemed to be superstitious. They had mistaken ideas about God and how to serve him. Nanak did his best to put them right as politely as possible.

Once, when he was on his travels across India, he came to the city of **Hardwar** by the holy River Ganges.

Nanak with his two helpers, Bala (a Hindu) and Mardana (a Muslim). Nanak wanted members of different religions to be friends. Mardana has the lute.

It was morning, and people had gone to wash and bathe in the river. As they stood in the river, they would pick up water in their hands and throw it towards the rising sun.

Nanak went down to the riverside and faced the other way, with his back to the sun. He bent down, picked up some water in his hands and threw it in the 'wrong' direction. The people were amazed. Was the stranger mad? They asked him: 'What do you think you are doing?' 'What do you think *you* are doing?' said Nanak. 'We throw water towards the sun for the sake of our ancestors who have died. They have gone to live in the other world, where the sun rises,' said the people.

Guru Nanak at the river.

Nanak smiled, walked back into the river, and went on throwing water towards the west, where the sun sets. Now the people began to grow really angry. Someone shouted: 'How dare you throw water in the wrong direction?'

'I live in the Punjab, west of here,' said Nanak. 'It's been very dry over there, so I'm sending some water to make my crops grow.' They laughed at him. 'Your water won't reach the Punjab!' they said.

'Yours won't reach the sun either,' he told them.

Nanak then explained that what they were doing was useless. The sun was not a god – it was something wonderful made by God. Instead of throwing water towards it, they would do much better to pray, work hard and help other people.

Part of a song by Guru Nanak

'Dirty hands may be washed
  with water,
Dirty clothes may be cleansed
  with soap.
A mind made dirty by sin and evil
Can only be cleansed by service
  to God.'
(Japji XV, simplified.)

Guru Nanak's birthday (4)

This unit tells you how Sikhs celebrate Guru Nanak's birthday.

Read around the clock! (The Akhand Path)

To celebrate **Guru** Nanak's birthday Sikhs hold a 'read-in' of their holy book. It takes about 48 hours to read the **Guru Granth Sahib** aloud from beginning to end. This takes place in the temple (**gurdwara**) and there are teams of readers who take it in turns. The holy book is written in an old and beautiful form of the Punjabi language. It takes a lot of time and hard work to become an expert reader.

You do not have to stay in the temple all the time. People can drop in, on their way home from school or work, for example. But often, when they get there, they find it so beautiful that they do not want to leave. Sikhs who go to the temple regularly know many of the songs by heart.

The Guru Granth Sahib

The holy book of the Sikhs is called the Guru Granth Sahib. It was compiled by the Fifth Guru, Arjan, in 1604. It is printed in Punjabi letters and always has 1,430 pages. It consists of 5,894 hymns, called **shabads**, each of which has a special tune, called a **raga**, in Indian music. Many of the hymns were composed by Guru Nanak himself. Some are the work of other gurus, and poems by non-Sikhs also find a place.

A Sikh conducting an Akhand Path.

Reading the scriptures in a temple.

Guru Nanak admired the work of Kabir, a Muslim poet and teacher, and a number of Kabir's songs are included. The hymns of the Guru Granth Sahib are sung in praise of God. They also teach people how to live together in peace and love. Sikhs believe that there is value in other religions, but for them the light of truth shines most brightly in the teaching of the Ten Gurus and the holy book.

How the holy book is treated

The Tenth Guru, Gobind **Singh**, declared that no human teacher would come after him. Instead the scriptures would serve as teacher for the Sikh community. So the holy book is treated as if it were a living person. It is kept on a bed in a special room in the temple and brought out in the morning with great respect. The book is placed on a raised platform with a decorated canopy above it. A man waves a **chauri** above it as the book is read aloud. A chauri is like a fly-whisk or fan. Sikhs bow low as they approach the scriptures and often make a present of money or perhaps milk, or bread or something else to eat. Later on these gifts may be used in the public dining hall (**langar**) which is attached to the temple.

'I ask You, O God, for nothing at any time but the love of Your pure name: grant it to me, O Bright One.
The pied cuckoo, Nanak, prays for the sweet water of Your name…
Grant me Your name as my wealth, so that I may wear it as a necklace on my heart.'

The pied cuckoo, or chatrick, is supposed to be a thirsty bird. In the same way, Nanak is thirsty to know more about God.

Sharing food – a sign of friendship

This unit tells you how important it is for
Sikhs to share food, and why.

*Sharing karah
parshad.*

When **Guru** Nanak was born people were divided in
many ways. There were two main religions:
Hinduism and Islam. Many people were also
divided, from birth, into different groups or **castes**.
The rich looked down on the poor and those who
belonged to the 'wrong' caste were often rejected by
others. Women were not thought to be equal to men.

How could people prove that they were united? One
way was to share food. That is why every Sikh
temple or **gurdwara** has a common dining hall to
which everyone is invited. Nobody is asked to pay.

Karah parshad

Sikhs also share special food at the end of their service. It is called **karah parshad**. Visitors are also offered karah parshad as a sign of friendship, even if there is no service going on. Sharing karah parshad is a way of saying 'We are all united in God'.

Karah parshad is served at the end of the Sikh service. Members of the congregation cup their hands together to receive a small portion. It is not forbidden to ask for more.

If karah parshad is not available then any other sensible food – nuts, sweets, fruit etc. – could be used as parshad. The idea of sharing is far more important than what is being shared.

How to make parshad

Ingredients

1 cup of sugar
1 cup of melted butter
1 cup of wholemeal flour

Method

1 Put the sugar with some water into a saucepan and simmer until the sugar has been dissolved.

2 Mix the butter and flour in another saucepan and fry until the flour is golden brown.

3 Add the sweet, warm water to the flour and cook on a low heat, stirring continuously until the mixture becomes very thick.

4 Leave to cool and set for at least half an hour.

The dining room (langar). Everyone is welcome.

A temple on wheels

This unit describes more festivities that celebrate Guru Nanak's birthday.

> **When the temple goes round the town we get to sit in the cab, next to the driver. You can see all the people waving. It's great!**
> – *Baldev*

In some places you can celebrate **Guru** Nanak's birthday by following a big model of the Golden Temple that stands at **Amritsar** in India. It is placed on the back of a big lorry and driven round the town. Skilled musicians sit inside, playing and singing the Guru's hymns. The yellow Sikh flags are carried in front and all kinds of clubs march behind.

A temple on wheels in a procession celebrating Guru Nanak's birthday.

Why the Golden Temple was built

Long ago there was a pool where, so some people say, Guru Nanak built a hut so that he could rest and pray in the course of his travels. A village grew up around the site, and here Guru Ram Das founded the city which is called Amritsar, or 'the pool of nectar'.

Later on, the pool was enlarged and the Golden Temple (**Harimandir**) was built. At that time Guru Arjan was the leader of the Sikhs. Work began in 1588, and the foundation stone was laid by Mian Mir, a friendly **Muslim**.

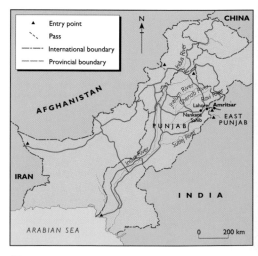

A map showing Amritsar.

How the Golden Temple teaches Sikh ideas

Guru Arjan wanted the Golden Temple to be open to everybody, so it was built with four doors, one on each side, instead of the usual single entrance. People in India were divided into **castes**: the Priests, the Warriors, the Traders and the Farmers. But the Guru wanted people to get away from the idea that one group was better than another. The Sikh scriptures record Guru Arjan's words: 'The four...are equal in learning about God'.

Something else is different about the Golden Temple. When you enter you have to go down, not up. This reminds you that you have to be humble when you think about God and pray to him.

The Harimandir was completed in 1604. Then the very first copy of the scriptures, the **Guru Granth Sahib**, was placed inside.

The Temple is built of marble, and stands in the centre of the sacred pool. The great dome and the upper walls are covered in gold leaf, which is how the Temple got its name. A wide causeway crosses the pool and leads to the Temple. There is a walkway on each side, and special rest rooms for the pilgrims who come from all over the world. People who are ill sometimes come to bathe in the water and pray for healing.

When the Harimandir was finished Guru Arjan composed these words:

> 'By repeating God's name I
>   have made God's temple...
> My house has been constructed
>   – my garden and tank have
>   been built: may God enter!
> O Nanak – there is no shelter
>   except in God...'

The Golden Temple in Amritsar.

Guru Gobind Singh's birthday (I)

This unit tells the story of the young Guru Gobind Singh.

Gobind **Singh** was the Tenth **Guru**. Sometimes he is called the 'Saint-Soldier'. He was born in Patna, in India, in the year 1666. For Sikhs he is second only to Guru Nanak. He organized the Sikh community in a new way, which has lasted right up to the present time. So his birthday is an important festival.

Gobind as a boy

Many stories are told about Gobind Rai, as he was called at first. He was ready to stand up for himself and his friends. In those days, people were expected to be very humble when the Governor came along. In fact, they had to fall down flat as he rode by with his fine followers. Gobind thought this was disgraceful – it was treating the Governor, the Emperor's servant, as if he were a god. So he persuaded his friends not to bow down. But one day they went a bit too far and, as the Governor rode past, shouted rude remarks at him. So Gobind got into trouble.

On another occasion, when he was practising with his bow and arrow, his friends challenged him to hit a moving target. A woman was coming along with a water-pot on her head. Gobind shot an arrow and smashed the pot to pieces. Of course the woman complained to Gobind's mother, who talked to him very seriously. 'If you want to hit moving targets,' she said, 'then go out into the forest and shoot at lions and leopards!'

▌ *Celebrating Gobind Singh's birthday.*

Gobind's father

Gobind's father was the Ninth Guru, Tegh Bahadur. He lived in dangerous times. The Emperor of India, Aurangzeb, believed that Islam was the only true religion. Unlike the previous Emperor, Akbar, he thought that people should be made to accept it, even by force. Guru Tegh Bahadur, the leader of the Sikhs, refused to obey, and his head was cut off in **Delhi** in 1675. The Emperor even commanded that nobody should bury his body. But a brave Sikh removed the head and took it back to **Anandpur**. There the young Gobind was proclaimed the Tenth Guru. His task was to lead the Sikhs in their fight for freedom.

Greetings on the Guru's birthday

When Sikhs send greeting cards to mark the Guru's birthday, they often quote these words:

Grant me in this, O Lord, that
I may never be afraid to do good deeds.
I should have no fear of the enemy when I go to
battle, and turn victory certainly to my side.
In my mind there is but one desire,
That I may ever be singing Your praises.
And when the time comes, I should die fighting
In the field of action!

Greeting card for Guru Gobind Singh's birthday

Guru Gobind Singh's birthday (2)

This unit tells you how music is used to celebrate the Guru's birthday and other occasions.

Music practice on tabla and harmonium.

Guru Gobind **Singh** was a very good poet and musician. He composed many hymns and songs. In the year 1734 his works were collected and made into a book, sometimes called 'The Granth of the Tenth Guru'. If you go to the Sikh temple on his birthday, is is very likely that you will hear some of them. Many Sikhs know them by heart.

Sikh instruments

You could say that Sikhism is a 'singalong' religion. People learn about God by listening to songs, learning them and joining in. Some boys and girls go to the temple or **gurdwara** during the week after school in order to have music lessons.

The most popular instrument is the harmonium. It is quite small – when you fold it up it looks just like a box – two feet long and one foot square. So you can take it with you even on a bus. Then you sit on the floor, open it up and use your left hand to work the bellows. This blows air into the harmonium. Air passes through the reeds inside the box when you play the notes with your right hand.

A dictionary of Sikh music

shabad – *a hymn from the holy book*

shabad kirtan - *sacred hymn-singing*

ragi – *an expert musician*

jorri – *another name for the tabla (pair of drums)*

baja – *another name for the harmonium (or any wind instrument)*

raga – *a hymn tune*

The harmonium has black and white notes just like a piano or keyboard. The scale is the same as on a piano, although the range is not as wide. It's quite easy to play a simple tune, but of course you have to practise hard to be really good.

Some people also go to the gurdwara to learn the **tabla**, a pair of special drums. They are made of wood, hollowed out, with one end covered in goat skin. One of the drums is narrow: you play it with your fingers. The other drum is broader, so that you can use your fingers, the flat of your hand or the hard part of your hand. Many different notes can be sounded – it all depends on the way you play. What's more, you have to play both drums at once, so it is not easy.

Using music to worship

The harmonium and tabla can be used for all kinds of music. But the Sikhs use them in a special way in praise of God. Each of the hymns in the holy scriptures has its own tune, called a **raga**. These tunes are linked with the time of day, some of them are thought more suitable for the morning, the afternoon, and so on.

On Guru Gobind Singh's birthday expert musicians sing hymns – his own work and those that are found in the **Guru Granth Sahib**. This is called **kirtan**, or sacred singing. They may use a special hymn book called **Amrit Kirtan** – 'The Sweetness of Singing'. One plays the drums while two others sing and play the harmonium. Sometimes the drummer joins in the singing, too.

Musicians playing kirtan.

Guru Gobind Singh's birthday (3)

This unit describes the symbol and flag used by Sikhs and explains why they are important.

The Khanda symbol.

The flag and the emblem

Sikhs often send greeting cards to celebrate the birthday of **Guru** Gobind **Singh**. Each card usually shows the Sikh emblem, the **Khanda**, which reminds people of what the Guru stood for. The emblem also appears on the yellow banner of the Sikhs which flies outside each temple.

What the Khanda means

At the centre of the Khanda is the two-edged sword. This is also called Khanda and it represents the One True God. Nobody can describe God, so you have to use picture-language about him. The two-edged sword stands for God the creator, who can destroy as well. Guru Gobind Singh gave God the name 'All-steel', because steel is the hardest and sharpest of metals.

The second part of the emblem is the **chakkar**, or circle. A circle has no end, so it reminds us of eternity. In the same way, God has no beginning or end. A ring can also be seen as a fence, so the chakkar reminds the Sikhs to keep within the rules of their religion.

The third part of the emblem consists of two curved swords called **kirpans**. One of them stands for 'piri', or spiritual power, and the other for 'miri', or political power (power in the world).

Spiritual power is the help from God which people need in order to live a good life and, in the end, to be united with God for ever. Sikhs believe that they can have this power by obeying the teaching of the Ten Gurus and the holy book.

The Pingalwara in Amritsar

When Bhagat Puran Singh was a young man he picked up a disabled baby who had been abandoned. For many years he carried the disabled person on his back, and later on a bicycle. He also set up homes for the disabled (Pingalwara). This is piri, or spiritual power, in action.

'Power in this world' (miri) could mean that Sikhs should have their own independent country and their own government. In his day, Guru Gobind Singh fought against the Emperor, who ruled from **Delhi**, and in the 19th century the Maharajah (King) Ranjit Singh ruled over an empire from his capital in **Amritsar**. Nowadays some Sikhs think they should have a country of their own, separate from India, to be called **Khalistan**, 'the land of the pure'. But most Sikhs would like to play their part in helping everybody to live happily together in peace and friendship. They fight for their rights and for other people, too. So 'power in the world' can mean 'power to play a helpful part'.

'All humans are the same, though they appear different.
The bright and the dark, the ugly and the beautiful.
All human beings have the same eyes, the same ears...
All human beings are the reflections of the same Lord.'
(Guru Gobind Singh, *Saint-Soldier*, page 64.)

Bhagat Puran Singh helps the destitute.

Baisakhi (1): the five friends

This unit tells you how the festival of Baisakhi remembers the first five members of the Sikh community.

Guru Gobind Singh with the Five Beloved at Anandpur.

What is Baisakhi?

Baisakhi is probably the most important of all Sikh festivals. It was on this day that **Guru** Gobind **Singh** set up the **Khalsa**, the community of Sikhs who are ready to give everything for God. Sikhs will organise a special procession – usually on 14 April – to mark Baisakhi. At the front of the procession you will see five men, dressed in saffron-coloured (yellow) robes and turbans and carrying shining swords. These are the Five Beloved, five friends who remind us of what happened long ago in the city of **Anandpur**.

How the Five Beloved were chosen

It was New Year's Day (Baisakhi) in the year 1699. Thousands of Sikhs had come from far and wide to meet their Guru, Gobind Singh. The Sikh community was under attack, and many of them were worried about the future.

At last Guru Gobind Singh appeared, dressed in saffron yellow, with a blue sash. He carried a long sword.

'Who is ready to give up everything for God?' he cried. 'I want someone who is ready to give his head!'

People were silent. Nobody moved. But at last Daya Ram came forward. He was a shopkeeper from Lahore. 'I am ready!' he declared. 'So take my head!'

The Guru took Daya Ram inside the tent and then came out again. His sword was dripping with blood. People were horrified.

'I want a second Sikh' said Gobind Singh 'who is also ready to offer his head.'

At last Dharam Das came forward. He was a farmer from **Delhi**. He too went into the tent and did not reappear. He was followed by Mokhan Chand, a washerman and Sahib Chand, a barber. Last of all was Himmat Rai, a water carrier. Each came from a different **caste** or group. What had happened to them? Had the Guru killed them? Or had he cut off the heads of five goats instead?

Shock turned into amazement and delight when Guru Gobind Singh reappeared – not with a blood-stained sword, but with the five volunteers – alive! They too were dressed in bright saffron yellow robes and wearing turbans.

'These brave men were ready to risk everything' said the Guru. 'They are now the Five Beloved – soldiers and saints. They are the first members of the **Khalsa**, the new fellowship of the Sikhs!'

'He who thinks of no one but the true God…
in whose heart the light of the Perfect One shines…
Only he can be recognized as a pure member of the Khalsa.'

The Five Beloved in a modern procession.

Baisakhi (2): the turban and the Five Ks

This unit tells you about the Sikh 'uniform' and the Amrit ceremony.

After **Guru** Gobind **Singh** had chosen the Five Beloved at **Baisakhi** in the year 1699, he gave them a special uniform: the Five Ks. Every Sikh who follows in the footsteps of the Five Beloved must take part in the **Amrit** ceremony to be baptized as a Sikh and wear the Five Ks: **kesh**, **kangha**, **kara**, **kachera** and **kirpan**.

Kesh

Kesh means 'uncut hair'. Sikhs who really want to practise their religion do not cut their hair. They believe that God has given them hair as a crown. Sikhs with uncut hair show that they trust in God and want to obey him. Of course, the hair must be kept clean and tidy – that is why it is covered with a cloth or turban.

The five Ks.
1 Kesh
2 Kangha
3 Kara
4 Kachera
5 Kirpan.

Kangha

The second K is kangha, which means 'comb'. It helps to keep the hair clean and tidy. It also reminds Sikhs to keep their souls clean and honest, as well, by remembering to pray, both aloud and silently in the mind. It reminds Sikhs to think about the Name of God and about God's mysterious power and goodness.

Kara

The third K is kara, a bracelet made of steel and worn on the right wrist. It is shaped in a circle with no end and so reminds Sikhs that their link with God should never end. It is made of steel, not gold, to remind Sikhs to be strict with themselves and not greedy for riches.

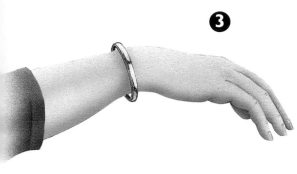

Another meaning is that a circle can act like a fence. It reminds Sikhs to keep the rules of good behaviour and not give in to wrong thoughts and ideas. With the steel bracelet on their wrist, how could they steal or strike someone weaker than themselves?

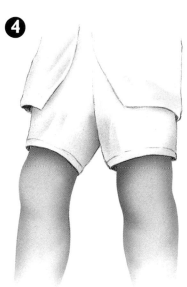

Kachera

The fourth K is kachera, a special pair of shorts. You can run, march or swim in them without any difficulty. Guru Gobind Singh wanted members of the **Khalsa** to be trained soldiers, well behaved and ready to fight only for a good cause.

Kirpan

The fifth K is the kirpan, a kind of sword about six to nine inches long. This is worn on the body. Some people wear a miniature kirpan instead. Those who wear the kirpan are reminded that they gain power and freedom through serving God.

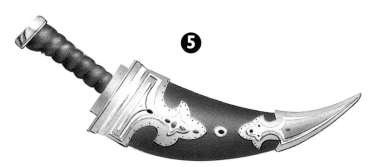

Baisakhi (3): Amrit

This unit describes how Sikhs are baptized at the Amrit ceremony.

> **I was baptized when I was 17. I had started to wear the Five Ks when I was 15, and I wore them through College. Being a baptized Sikh is a strict way of life. You have to pray night and morning and take a bath. You can't drink alcohol or smoke. I don't eat meat either – even though the scriptures don't actually forbid it.**
>
> *– Raji*

Raji's **kirpan** is a small one, hanging over her shoulder on a band. 'It's easier for work' she says. Along with others, Raji took part in the Amrit ceremony during the festival of **Baisakhi** – just like the first Five Beloved nearly 300 years ago. **Amrit** is often called Sikh baptism.

The Amrit ceremony

You have to be at least 14 to join the **Khalsa**. Five Sikhs are chosen to represent the original five of 1699. They kneel down and each one takes it in turn to stir sugar and water in a bowl with the two-edged sword, the **Khanda**. There are prayers, readings from the scripture and the poems of **Guru** Gobind **Singh**.

Then the sweet sugar water (called amrit) is sprinkled five times on the hair, eyes and hands of each new member, who says in Punjabi: 'The Khalsa belongs to God!' and 'Victory belongs to God!'

A Sikh baptism – the Amrit ceremony.

They are then members of the Sikh Khalsa, and have promised to follow the teaching of the Gurus, to worship one God only, to keep the law of marriage and not to use magic spells or charms.

The new members are given new names. Men are called '**Singh**', which means 'lion' and women are called '**Kaur**', which means 'princess'.

Being in the Khalsa

Is it boring or difficult to belong to the Khalsa? 'A lot depends on who you are with' says Raji. 'I used to be more into the pop world, though not totally into discos.' What about the daily prayers lasting over 20 minutes? 'There are cassettes which can be played with the prayers. If I'm down I'll listen to them.'

What do Sikhs believe?

Not all Sikhs belong to the Khalsa. To be a Sikh you must:

- believe in one God;
- accept the teaching of the Ten Gurus;
- believe in the **Guru Granth Sahib**;
- accept the importance of Sikh baptism, even if not baptized yourself;
- not belong to any other religion.

Baisakhi (4): washing the flag pole

This unit is about the importance of the Sikh flag and the way it is used at Baisakhi.

Taking down the flag pole.

Baisakhi is an Indian New Year festival. It comes round on 13 or 14 April. A New Year means a new beginning, so it is time to wash the flag pole that stands outside each Sikh temple. This is great fun, and also a sign of faith.

The flag

The flag, called **Nishan Sahib**, is triangular and bright saffron yellow. It was given to the Sikhs by the Sixth **Guru**, Har Gobind, to encourage them in battle. Har Gobind also commanded that every **gurdwara** should have a big kettledrum, which is beaten on special occasions.

Nowadays the Nishan Sahib flies from the top of a tall steel pole. The pole is also wrapped in yellow cloth. Every year, when Baisakhi comes round, it is time to take the pole down and wash it. People come from far and wide for this great event.

Taking down the pole

Taking down a flag pole is a tricky job. Some strong men – members of the **Khalsa** – go up to the temple roof and undo the fastenings that hold the pole upright. Then, slowly and carefully, with many willing hands helping, it is lowered to the ground. Next it is laid on some long tables. After that, members of the temple take off the yellow coverings that have protected the pole since last year.

Washing the pole

Then the pole is washed with yoghurt. Sikhs feel that this is the purest substance that you can find. Girls and boys can join in with the washing of the pole. People enjoy themselves, and favourite hymns are sung. The lesson is clear: it is no use washing the pole unless you wash your soul free from sin as well!

Setting the pole up again

People have brought gifts – new yellow coverings to protect the pole for another year. When the washing is finished, they are tied on until the pole is covered from top to bottom. Any spare wrappings can be donated to use in the temple later. The old covers from last year are often cut up and taken home as souvenirs.

Soon there are loud cheers as the clean pole slowly goes up again, proudly wearing bright new wrappings, with the Nishan Sahib flying at the top. Everybody shouts: '**Waheguru!** Waheguru!' which means 'Victory is the Lord's!'

After that, everyone is invited to the **langar**, where there is tasty food to enjoy.

Washing the flag pole with yoghurt.

Baisakhi (5): bhangra dancing

This unit tells you about the kind of dancing that is enjoyed by Sikhs all over the world.

This is how a boy in Kent, England described his dancing practice:

> **When you are dancing in public you have to smile all the time. It's tough because your legs ache. When we practise we don't have to worry about smiling, but teacher tells us we ought to smile anyway.**
> – *Joginder*

How bhangra began

Nowadays the name 'bhangra' is given to a kind of pop music that combines Asian and European styles, but the original bhangra is a kind of folk dance. It began in the Punjab, in India.

The name 'Punjab' means 'Five Rivers'. It is the name given to the northern land where five rivers join to make the great River **Indus**. Part of the Punjab now belongs to India and part to Pakistan, so there is a province called 'Punjab' in both countries.

The Punjab is a good land – wheat grows well and most of the people are farmers. A bad harvest means poverty, but a good harvest means money in the farmer's pocket. So the farmers rejoice and relax when harvest festival time comes round. It is a time to sing and dance, and also to say 'thank you' to God for his goodness.

So, with money to spend, the farmer sets off for the fair, determined to have a good time and to celebrate **Baisakhi** in style. This is the theme of the original bhangra folk dancing, for which you need a dhol (a big barrel-shaped two-ended drum) and a good solo singer to inspire the dancers with folk songs and shouts of encouragement. Nowadays microphones and sound systems can make the music louder.

Jugnu celebrate Baisakhi.

How is bhangra performed?

Bhangra is performed by groups of men. They dance to tell the story of the farmer's life. They carry their tools to work in the fields, where they dig and dig and look up hopefully. No rain! Things look bad! How the farmers hope for rain! Then, suddenly, the rain comes and the earth soaks up water. Now the farmers are very happy. They begin to weed and cut the crop, and then, after a hard day's work, they go home. In the last part of the dance the farmer sets off for the fair, with a staff in his hand and money in his pockets. It's time to celebrate!

Where is bhangra performed?

Bhangra dancing is popular in India, and Sikhs have introduced it to other countries, as well. Bhangra dancers from Gravesend, England, have won prizes at the International Eisteddfod (music festival) in Llangollen, in Wales.

Musical instruments for bhangra
Algozai – *a pair of flutes*
Chimta – *a forked strip of metal making sounds rather like a tambourine*
Dhol – *a barrel-shaped, double ended drum*
Kaatto – *an instrument shaped like a bird, which gives a rhythmic beat*
Shikaa – *an instrument made of strips of wood, which produces a clapping sound*
Toombi - *an instrument like a violin, but with only one string, which you pluck with your finger*

The martyrdom of Guru Arjan (I)

This unit describes the way that Sikhs remember the story of Guru Arjan.

> **They put up a table outside the temple and gave away free drinks. We all got cans. I had a can of Coke.**
>
> – Navnendar

Free drinks being given out by Sikhs in memory of Guru Arjan.

Free drinks! Cool drinks!

Once a year, in June, Sikhs give away cold water and bottles of soft drinks. In India it is very hot at that time of year, so they go to railway stations, bus stops and markets. People of every religion are glad to have cool refreshment 'in the **Guru**'s name'!

In parts of India where canned drinks are dear or scarce, the people make sharbat, a mixture of water and milk, with ice to make it cool. A large tub of shabat is put out, and anyone can have a drink from it.

All this is in memory of the brave Guru Arjan. He had to suffer terribly. But he always kept calm and cool because of his faith in God. This is the message of the cool drinks.

The story of Guru Arjan

Arjan was the Fifth Guru. In his time, much of India was ruled by the Emperor Akbar, who was friendly to the Sikhs. Arjan was able to travel round the country preaching. New people joined the Sikh faith. The Golden Temple was built in **Amritsar** and the **Guru Granth Sahib** was compiled. The Emperor Akbar came to visit Guru Arjan, and gave his approval to the holy book of the Sikhs. 'There is nothing in it,' he said 'except love and devotion to God.'

But then Akbar died, and his son Jehangir became Emperor. Jehangir drove out his own brother Khusro, who fled towards Afghanistan. On the way he asked Guru Arjan for help. 'I have no money for princes,' said the Guru, 'I have money only for the poor. 'I *am* poor!' said the unfortunate Khusro, and so the Guru gave him 5,000 **rupees** to help him get away. But Khusro was caught by the Emperor's troops, and taken to **Delhi** in chains.

Now Guru Arjan's enemies whispered that he was a traitor, and that the holy book which he had compiled contained shameful attacks on the **Muslim** and **Hindu** religions. Guru Arjan was summoned to meet the Emperor Jehangir and explain himself. He knew he would soon be face to face with death.

Before he left Amritsar, he appointed his son Har Gobind as his successor and comforted his wife Ganga. In those days wives were sometimes expected to burn themselves to death on their husbands' funeral **pyres**. Guru Arjan forbade this. 'Live when I am gone!' he said.

This is the hymn that Guru Arjan sang to the Emperor Akbar:
One man invokes the god Ram,
Another Khuda.
Some bathe in the Ganges,
Others visit Mecca.
Some call themselves Hindus,
Others Muslims.
But he who recognizes God's will –
*   says Nanak –*
Will know the secret of the Lord
*   God.*

Guru Arjan reading the scriptures.

The martyrdom of Guru Arjan (2)

This unit continues the story of Guru Arjan and his cruel death.

The court of Emperor Jehangir.

The hymn of peace

Guru Arjan composed the hymn of peace, and Sikhs often use it at funerals:

O man, why are you slow to remember Him

By whose favour you wear jewels?

O man, never forget your God,

By whose favour you ride on horses and elephants.

Keep God in your heart,

By whose favour you have gardens and property and wealth;

Think about Him who is invisible

And He will preserve you in this world and the next.

The Emperor Jehangir was very angry with **Guru** Arjan. He asked him why he had helped Khusro, a traitor and an enemy.

'I did it because he was poor,' said Arjan, 'and not because he was your enemy. I also remembered the kindness of your late father, the Emperor Akbar.' Jehangir was not satisfied. He told Guru Arjan that he would have to pay a huge fine – 200,000 **rupees**.

'Whatever money I have is for the poor, the friendless and the stranger,' said Guru Arjan. 'I will give you money if you need it, but I cannot pay a fine. If I did that I would admit that I had committed a crime.'

Then the Emperor demanded that any words which spoke evil of the **Hindu** or **Muslim** religions should be rubbed out of the holy book. Guru Arjan replied that the hymns of the Sikhs did not criticize any religion. They were written in praise of the One True God.

Guru Arjan's punishment

Some Sikhs in the city of Lahore wanted to save the Guru by collecting money and paying the fine, but Arjan forbade them to do it. Fines were only paid by slanderers and robbers, and not one word of the scriptures could be altered. 'The **Guru Granth Sahib**' he said, 'has been compiled to bring happiness and not misery in this world and the next.'

Next Arjan was tortured: red-hot sand was poured over him and he was soaked in boiling water. But he did not give in or curse his enemies. Instead he kept very calm. 'The heated cauldron has become cold,' he said. 'God is the strength of the strengthless.'

Guru Arjan was a martyr. He died for his faith. Some say that they killed him at last and threw his body into the River Ravi. But others tell how he bathed himself in its ice-cold waters, recited the **Japji** prayer, and died. This was in the month of June, 1606.

And that is why Sikhs give away free cool drinks every year in June.

What did Guru Arjan leave behind?

Guru Arjan left behind him:
- *the **Harimandir**, the Golden Temple, to visit and worship;*
- *the Guru Granth Sahib, the holy book, to read and learn;*
- *songs to sing in praise of God.*

Guru Arjan at peace as he faces death.

39

Divali

This unit tells you about the Sikh Festival of Light.

Some Sikhs in England were asked to try and describe **Divali**.

> ❝ **Amritsar looks just like Blackpool! The Holy City is lit up with multicoloured lights.** ❞
> – *Baldev*

> ❝ **The Golden Temple becomes a floating palace of multicoloured lights.** ❞
> – *Jastinder*

> ❝ **Divali comes just after Guy Fawkes Night (5 November). We have a lighted candle in the house, and sparklers. My dad lets the fireworks off.** ❞
> – *Nasib*

The Golden Temple at Amritsar at Divali time.

A story for Divali

Sikhs have a story of their own to tell at Divali time. It recalls the bravery of Har Gobind, the Sixth **Guru**.

He led the Sikhs in the 17th century, at a time when the Emperor Jehangir ruled over much of India. Jehangir's armies had overthrown many kings and princes (rajahs) and put them in prison at **Gwalior Fort**. There they suffered badly. The food was poor and they were dressed in rags.

The Emperor also came to suspect that Guru Har Gobind was plotting against him. So he too was arrested and sent to Gwalior. The charge was treason and the punishment could be death.

While he was in the fort, Har Gobind did his best to help his fellow prisoners. He got clean clothes and better food for them. His enemies did their worst – trying to kill him and to poison the mind of the Emperor against him. But in the end they failed, and orders came for Guru Har Gobind to be released.

Guru Har Gobind is released from Gwalior Fort.

Har Gobind's release

But what about the poor princes left in prison? Har Gobind declared that he would not leave unless they were let out, too. The Emperor replied that he could take as many as could cling to his coat but the rest would have to stay. At this, so the story goes, Guru Har Gobind sent for a coat with long tassels. All 52 princes were able to cling on somehow, and all 52 gained their freedom. Guru Har Gobind had got the better of the Emperor! He returned to **Amritsar** in triumph. It was Divali time, and the city was gleaming with candles and oil lamps. Ever since then those lights (and the modern electric illuminations, too) have a special meaning for the Sikh: they celebrate freedom.

Hola Mohalla

This unit explains why sport and fitness are important to Sikhs.

▌ *A kabaddi game in progress.*

❝ **We hope to have a kabaddi league soon. We're playing other schools in the town. You have two teams in kabaddi. One person tries to break through and the others try to tig him. He has to hold his breath and keep saying 'kabaddi' for as long as he can.**
– *Baldev* ❞

Sikhs like sport. They enjoy the Indian game of **kabaddi** and also football. In England, for example, there are plenty of **Guru** Nanak football teams in different towns. Sometimes the temple may set up a sports hall and encourage basketball and other games. This sporting ideal goes back to Guru Gobind **Singh**, who thought that the Sikhs ought to keep fit. This is commemorated every year in the festival of **Hola Mohalla**.

How did Hola Mohalla begin?

In India the festival of Holi celebrates the coming of spring. It gives everyone a chance to relax and enjoy themselves. People throw coloured water over each other.

Long ago, Guru Gobind Singh thought that Holi was an excuse for hooliganism. Sikhs should do something better, he thought, and Holi should become Hola Mohalla – practise on the battlefield. So he summoned his supporters to meet him at **Anandpur**.

Instead of drinking too much and soaking each other's clothes, they were to take part in a drill, parades and mock battles. There were competitions in archery and wrestling, as well as in music and poetry. At the end Guru Gobind Singh led an attack on a model castle, specially built for the occasion. This would help the Sikhs to be ready to face any attack from the troops of the Emperor Aurungzeb.

Hola Mohalla at Anandpur.

What happens today?

Hola Mohalla is still celebrated at Anandpur. For many years the descendants of Guru Gobind Singh would ride past on their elephants. Not any more! But there is still a great carnival at Anandpur, with a procession of yellow banners (**Nishan Sahib**) and free hospitality at the **langar**.

Outside India, far away from Anandpur, there will be another **Akhand Path**, as well as talks about the teaching of Gobind Singh. His poems will be recited and his songs sung.

Sikhs have kept up the Guru's tradition. Many of them have served in the Indian army, both before and after India became independent, and they still think it is a good idea to encourage sport, especially for young men. So sometimes the temple may set up a sports complex, and the Guru Nanak football team may compete in the local league.

Sikhs should be good sportsmen and sportswomen. They are expected to remember that the Guru said:

'I will make sparrows hunt down hawks;
I will turn jackals into fierce lions
And make one Sikh fight a legion'.
(Saint-Soldier, page 9.)

Glossary

Akhand Path A non-stop reading of the Scriptures

Amrit 1 The ceremony which takes place when a Sikh becomes a member of the Khalsa. Often called 'Sikh baptism'.
2 Nectar: a mixture of sugar and water used in the amrit ceremony

Amritsar A city in India – home of the Golden Temple

Amrit Kirtan 'The Sweetness of Singing'. This is a special hymn book that may be used on Guru Gobind Singh's birthday.

Anandpur A city in India – where Gobind Singh was proclaimed the Tenth Guru

Astrologer Someone who seeks to find meaning in the movements of the stars

Baisakhi The Sikh New Year Festival (in April)

Bein A river in India – where Guru Nanak had a vision of God

Bhagat Someone who is totally devoted to God: a saint

Caste A division of people in India; traditionally there are four castes: Priests, Warriors, Traders and Farmers. The Sikh religion tries to overcome caste divisions

Chakkar A circle – at the centre of the Sikh emblem, or Khanda

Chauri A whisk that is waved above the Sikh Scriptures while they are read aloud

Delhi A great city in India, once the capital of the Mogul Emperor

Divali The Festival of Light

Gurdwara A Sikh place of worship. It means 'the doorway to the Guru'

Gurmukhi An old and beautiful form of the Punjabi language, in which the scriptures are written

Guru Teacher. In Sikhism this word refers to the Ten (human) Gurus and also the Guru Granth Sahib

Guru Granth Sahib The Sikh Scriptures or Holy Book

Gwalior Fort A place where Guru Hargobind was put in prison

Hardwar A city in India – visited by Guru Nanak

Harimandir The Golden Temple in Amritsar

Hindu Someone who follows the majority religion of India

Hola Mohalla A festival that recalls how Guru Gobind Singh trained his army

Indus A great river in India, which flows through the Punjab

Japji An important set of prayers, recited by Sikhs

Kabaddi An Indian game, in which players try to catch one another

Kachera Undershorts: one of the Five Ks

Kangha Comb: one of the Five Ks

Kara Steel bracelet: one of the Five Ks

Karah parshad Food offered to God and then shared

Kaur Princess: name given to a woman member of the Khalsa

Khalistan 'Land of the Pure' – the independent homeland which some Sikhs would like to have

Kesh (Uncut) hair: one of the Five Ks

Khalsa The Community of the Pure: the Sikh community

Khanda A two-edged sword used in baptism and found in the Sikh emblem. Also used for the emblem itself

Kirpan Small sword: one of the Five Ks

Kirtan Singing hymns together

Langar The common dining-hall in a Sikh gurdwara

Mool Mantar Basic Teaching: a short statement found at the beginning of the Guru Granth Sahib

Muslim Someone who follows the faith and teaching of the prophet Mohammed

Nishan Sahib The Sikh flag

Pyre A fire on which dead bodies are burned

Raga A hymn tune

Ragi A musician who sings hymns from the Guru Granth Sahib

Rupees Indian coins

Sanskrit The ancient language of India

Shabad A hymn in the Guru Granth Sahib

Singh 'Lion': name given to a male member of the Khalsa

Tabla A pair of drums played with the hands

Talwandi Guru Nanak's birthplace – now called Nankana Sahib

Waheguru 'Wonderful Lord!' – Sikhs often say this during prayer and worship

Further reading

Sikhism. Nikky-Guninder Kaur Singh; Facts on File, 1993.

The Sikh World. Daljit Singh and Angela Smith; Macdonald & Co., 1985.

Sikhs and Sikhism. Sukhbir S Kapoor; Wayland (Publishers) Ltd, 1982.

World Religions: Sikhism. Kanwalijit Kaur-Singh; Wayland (Publishers) Ltd, 1995.

Religions through Festivals:Sikhism. Davinder Kaur Babraa; Longman, 1989.

Discovering Religions: Sikhism. ed. Sue Penney; Heinemann Publishers (Oxford) Ltd, 1995

Discovering Sacred Texts: The Guru Granth Sahib. Piara Singh Sambhi, ed. W. Owen Cole; Heinemann Publishers (Oxford) Ltd, 1994.

Let's Celebrate Spring. Mike Rosen, ed. Deb Elliott; Wayland (Publishers) Ltd, 1994.

Let's Celebrate Summer. Mike Rosen, ed. Deb Elliott; Wayland (Publishers) Ltd, 1994.

Let's Celebrate Autumn. Mike Rosen, ed. Deb Elliott; Wayland (Publishers) Ltd, 1994.

Let's Celebrate Winter. Mike Rosen, ed. Deb Elliott; Wayland (Publishers) Ltd, 1994.

Understanding Religions: Food and Fasting. Deidre Burke, Wayland (Publishers) Ltd, 1992.

Understanding Religions: Pilgrimages and Journeys. Katherine Prior, Wayland (Publishers) Ltd, 1992.

A closer look

This picture shows Hola Mohalla at Anandpur. Hola Mohalla is held during the festival of Holi, at the beginning of spring. Guru Gobind Singh started Hola Mohalla, practice on the battlefield, so that Sikhs could keep fit and would be ready to face any attack from the troops of the Emperor Aurangzeb. Hola Mohalla is still celebrated at Anandpur with a great carnival, a procession of yellow banners and free hospitality at the langar.

Index

Plain numbers (3) refer to the text. Italic numbers (*3*) refer to a picture.